Railroad Pennsylvania

Florida

Winter pleasure tours under the personally-conducted system of the

Pennsylvania railroad, Season of 1898. Vol. 1

Railroad Pennsylvania

Florida
Winter pleasure tours under the personally-conducted system of the Pennsylvania railroad, Season of 1898. Vol. 1

ISBN/EAN: 9783337257026

Printed in Europe, USA, Canada, Australia, Japan

Cover: Foto ©Andreas Hilbeck / pixelio.de

More available books at **www.hansebooks.com**

FLORIDA.

◂•▸

WINTER PLEASURE TOURS

UNDER THE PERSONALLY-CONDUCTED SYSTEM

OF THE

PENNSYLVANIA RAILROAD.

◂•▸

SPECIAL TRAINS OF PULLMAN VESTIBULE DRAWING-ROOM
SLEEPING AND DINING CARS.

SEASON OF 1898.

R. WOOD,
Gen'l Passenger Agent.

GEO. W. BOYD,
Ass't Gen'l Passenger Agent.

Allen, Lane & Scott, Printers.

PENNSYLVANIA TOURS

TO

FLORIDA.

◆

Winter and Spring of 1898.

◆

LORIDA is looked upon with great favor by the large number of people who feel the need of a midwinter as well as a midsummer holiday, and they find under its genial skies the rest and recreation which a working world makes necessary. To these people the personally-conducted tours of the Pennsylvania Railroad especially commend themselves. These tours are planned just to fit the two weeks' vacation which almost every one may take. The excursion rates are most liberal, and the style of traveling is first class in every particular. If the general sentiment concerning them is to be taken as an index of their popularity, they may in all verity be styled the ideal short winter tours.

The Pennsylvania Railroad Company, for the season of 1898, presents a series of four tours. They will be carried out under the personally-conducted system for which that company has become famous, and every detail relating to them will be maintained on that high grade which has been the marked characteristic of previous undertakings of this kind.

Arrangements so comprehensive and complete present a rare opportunity for recreation and pleasure on desirable dates.

THE DAYS OF STARTING AND RETURNING.

A series of four tours from Boston, New York, Philadelphia, Baltimore, Washington, and other principal points on the Pennsylvania System is fixed for the following dates :—

Leave New York, Tuesday, January 25,
Leave New York Tuesday, February 8,
Leave New York, Tuesday, February 22,
Leave New York, Tuesday, March 8, 1898.

Dates for leaving Boston are one day earlier in each instance.

The first three tours will each admit of a visit of TWO WHOLE WEEKS in the Flowery State, and the returning parties will leave Jacksonville for home on the dates following :—

First Tour, Thursday, February 10,
Second Tour, Thursday, February 24,
Third Tour, Thursday, March 10, 1898.

Tickets for the FOURTH TOUR are valid for return until MAY 31, 1898, by regular trains.

The period allowed is amply sufficient to admit of a thorough tour of all the interesting places in the Peninsula.

UNDER PERSONAL ESCORT.

Undoubtedly one of the most original and highly satis-factory creations of the Pennsylvania Railroad is the in-auguration of personally-conducted tours under the super-vision and direction of a Tourist Agent and Chaperon. The former, a man of broad experience, makes all arrange-ments that may be required, has a perfect knowledge of all routes, attends to the prompt movement of the train, and in every way looks to the comfort and enjoyment of his fellow-travelers.

The Chaperon, entirely an original conception of the Pennsylvania Railroad, has especial charge of ladies, par-ticularly those unaccompanied by parents or escort, min-istering to their necessities in a most intelligent manner, as experience has thoroughly educated her in the intrica-cies of railway travel and usage.

In the Chaperon the ladies find both a companion and guide. While furnishing all information that one could wish, and looking with watchful eyes after the comfort and pleasure of those in her charge, the Chaperon also stands to unescorted ladies in the exact relation that her title implies.

DISTINCTIVE FEATURES.

The marked success and popularity of the Pennsylvania Railroad Tours to Florida are due to several causes. The complete appointment of the special trains, the liberality of the rates and the return limit of tickets, are features that have attracted the traveling public ; but the most popular characteristic of these tours is the freedom of movement al-lowed the tourists after their arrival at destination. No fixed programme is set for them in Florida, but having arrived at Jacksonville they are at perfect liberty to dispose of their time as they see fit. They may travel over the State individually or in small parties, may stop wherever they choose and stay as long as is desirable, only keeping in view the return date, and arranging their migrations so as to be in Jacksonville in time to take the special train for home on the date fixed for its departure. This plan imposes on the tourists no compulsory conditions as to their movements, and at the same time secures to them all the benefits of the personally-conducted system.

HOW THE TOURISTS TRAVEL.

Each party will be transported from New York to Jacksonville in a special train of Pullman Vestibule Sleeping and Dining Cars. The train will be in direct charge of the Tourist Agent, who, aided by the Chaperon, will relieve the tourists of all the incidental cares of a long trip. The train will run through on a fast schedule in both directions.

The route of the tours of January 25 and February 22 is via Pennsylvania Railroad to Quantico, the Richmond, Fredericksburg and Potomac Railroad to Richmond, the Atlantic Coast Line to Ashley Junction, and the Plant System to Jacksonville; and that of the tours of February 8 and March 8 is via the Pennsylvania Railroad to Washington, Southern Railway to Columbia, and Florida Central and Peninsular Railroad to Jacksonville. Returning, the parties will travel by the same route as that used south-bound.

The dining-car feature is a most desirable one, and cannot fail to enlist the appreciation of all travelers, insuring comfortable meals at regular hours with ample time to enjoy them. All the meals necessary *en route* will be served in the dining car, the expense of the same being covered by the price of the tickets. Hours observed for meals will be :—

Breakfast . . . . 7.00 to 8.30 A. M.
Luncheon . . . . 12.30 to 1.30 P. M.
Dinner . . . . 6.00 to 7.30 P. M.

THE RATES AND CONDITIONS OF THE TICKETS.

The excursion tickets for these tours will be sold from Boston at $65.00, New York $50.00, Philadelphia $48.00, and from other stations named on other pages in this pamphlet at the rates there quoted. The price of the tickets includes railway transportation, and, for the first three tours, Pullman sleeping-car accommodations (one berth) and meals *en route* in both directions while traveling on the special train. The rate from Boston includes, in addition to above, berth from Boston to Philadelphia and return ; breakfast going and supper returning, at Broad Street Station, Philadelphia. The tickets will be accepted for passage only on the special train. They must be used for the return trip only on the special train appointed to leave Jacksonville on the date fixed for the return of the particular tour in question, except that as stated on page 6 tickets for the fourth tour will be valid returning by regular trains until May 31, 1897, and cover Pullman accommodations (one berth) and meals *on going trip* only ; nothing but transportation is included returning.

Tickets sold at points on this company's lines not reached by the special train cover transportation by regular trains to nearest junction point with the special train.

The tourists, upon reaching Jacksonville, will be left to pursue their own course until the return date, when they will take the special train at that point for the homeward trip.

WINTER IN FLORIDA.

Baggage should be checked through to Jacksonville via the route of tour selected.

The company reserves the right to attach special cars to regular trains, if, from any cause, the number of the party should be too small to warrant the running of a special train.

A SUGGESTION.

The number of persons for which accommodations can be provided on a special train of Pullman drawing-room cars is necessarily limited. It is prudent, therefore, that those who desire to join the party should make early application for tickets, and register their names for sleeping-car accommodations.

Tickets or itineraries may be secured at the ticket offices of the Pennsylvania Railroad Company in Boston, New York, Jersey City, Newark, Elizabeth, Trenton, Philadelphia, Wilmington, Baltimore, Washington, and the other stations from which rates are quoted, or by addressing

GEO. W. BOYD,
Assistant General Passenger Agent
Pennsylvania Railroad Co.,
BROAD STREET STATION, PHILADELPHIA, PA.

Special booking offices for personally-conducted tours have been established at the following offices, where representatives of the Tourist Bureau will be stationed:—

1196 Broadway,
New York City.

205 Washington Street,
Boston, Mass.

789 Broad Street,
Newark, N. J.

860 Fulton Street,
Brooklyn, N. Y.

Room 411, Broad St. Station, Philadelphia, Pa.

15th and G Streets,
Washington, D. C.

N. E. Corner Baltimore and Calvert Streets,
Baltimore, Md.

Corner Fifth Avenue and Smithfield Streets,
Pittsburg, Pa.

ROUND-TRIP RATES.

Altoona, Pa.	$50 65		Hamburg, Pa.	$50 00
Atlantic City, N. J.	49 25		Harrington, Del.	49 00
Baltimore, Md.	48 00		Harrisburg, Pa.	48 00
Bellefonte, Pa., via Tyrone	51 00		Havre de Grace, Md.	48 00
Belvidere, N. J.	50 00		Huntingdon, Pa.	50 00
Birdsboro, Pa.	49 35		Indiana, Pa.	52 30
Blairsville, Pa.	52 00		Irvineton, Pa.	53 65
Bordentown, N. J.	49 00			
Boston, Mass.	65 00		Jamesburg, N. J.	50 00
Bridgeton, N. J.	49 00		Jersey City, N. J.	50 00
Bristol, Pa.	48 80		Johnstown, Pa.	51 45
Bryn Mawr, Pa.	48 00		Kane, Pa.	52 95
Burlington, N. J.	48 60		Lambertville, N. J.	49 80
Canandaigua, N. Y.	52 85		Lancaster, Pa.	48 00
Cape May, N. J.	49 75		Latrobe, Pa.	52 20
Centreville, Md.	49 00		Lewistown Junction, Pa.	49 25
Chestnut Hill, Pa.	48 30		Lock Haven, Pa.	50 40
Chester, Pa.	48 00		Long Branch, N. J.	50 00
Clayton, Del.	48 40			
Clearfield, Pa.	51 20		Mt. Carmel, Pa.	49 65
Coatesville, Pa.	48 00		Mt. Union, Pa.	49 75
Columbia, Pa.	48 00		Manayunk, Pa.	48 25
Conewago, Pa.	48 00		Media, Pa.	48 00
Connellsville, Pa.	52 90		Merchantville, N. J.	48 20
Conshohocken, Pa.	48 50		Middletown, Del.	48 25
Corry, Pa.	54 10		Middletown, Pa.	48 00
			Milford, Del.	49 00
Dover, Del.	48 50		Millville, N. J.	49 00
Downingtown, Pa.	48 00		Milton, Pa.	49 35
Delmar, Del.	49 00		Moorestown, N. J.	48 50
Driftwood, Pa.	51 50		Mt. Holly, N. J.	48 70
			Mt. Joy, Pa.	48 00
Elizabeth, N. J.	50 00		Muncy, Pa.	49 65
Elkton, Md.	48 00			
Elmira, N. Y.	51 45		Nanticoke, Pa.	50 25
Emporium, Pa.	51 85		Newark, Del.	48 00
Erie, Pa.	54 85		Newark, N. J.	50 00
Frankford, Pa.	48 25		New Brunswick, N. J.	50 00
Freehold, N. J.	50 00		New Castle, Del.	48 00
			New York, N. Y.	50 00
Greensburg, Pa.	52 40		Norristown, Pa.	48 65
Germantown, Pa.	48 20		Northumberland, Pa.	49 15
Glassboro, N. J.	48 75			

Ocean Grove, N. J.	$50 00	Shamokin, Pa.	$49 50
Oxford, Pa.	48 00	Shenandoah, Pa.	50 00
		Spring City, Pa.	49 30
Perryville, Md.	48 00	Sunbury, Pa.	49 10
Perth Amboy, N. J.	50 00		
Philadelphia, Pa.	48 00	Trenton, N. J.	49 00
Phillipsburg, N. J.	50 00	Tulpohocken, Pa.	48 20
Phœnixville, Pa.	49 00	Tyrone, Pa.	50 40
Pittsburg, Pa.	53 00	Uniontown, Pa.	53 00
Pottstown, Pa.	49 00	Vineland, N. J.	49 00
Pottsville, Pa.	50 00		
Princeton, N. J.	49 60	Warren, Pa.	53 55
		Washington, D. C.	48 00
Rahway, N. J.	50 00	Watkins, N. Y.	51 95
Reading, Pa.	50 00	West Chester, Pa.	48 00
Red Bank, N. J.	50 00	Wilkesbarre, Pa.	50 35
Renovo, Pa.	50 95	Williamsport, Pa.	50 00
Rochester, N. Y.	54 00	Wilmington, Del.	48 00
		Wissahickon Heights, Pa.	48 30
Salem, N. J.	49 00	Woodbury, N. J.	48 30
Schuylkill Haven, Pa.	50 00	York, Pa.	48 00
Seaford, Del.	49 00		

Rates via Market Street Wharf do not include transfer of passenger or baggage through Philadelphia.

Half-tickets for use of children between five and twelve years of age will be sold at two-thirds above rates.

EXTRA PULLMAN ACCOMMODATIONS.

As previously stated, these rates include one double berth in sleeper, but in case extra Pullman accommodations are desired a limited number of persons can be furnished therewith at the following additional charges for the round trip from New York or Philadelphia :—

For entire section occupied by one person $13 00
For drawing-room occupied by one person 35 00
For drawing-room occupied by two persons 22 00
For drawing-room occupied by three persons 9 00

It should be borne in mind that the above are the *total* additional charges, so that in the case of drawing-room occupied by two persons the *per capita* charge is $11.00, and when occupied by three persons the *per capita* charge is $3.00.

For the fourth tour, where Pullman accommodations are furnished south-bound only, the charges for extra Pullman space will be one-half of above amounts.

ITINERARY IN DETAIL.

VIA ATLANTIC COAST LINE AND PLANT SYSTEM.

◂◆▸

SOUTH-BOUND SCHEDULE.

JANUARY 24 and FEBRUARY 21, 1898.

Eastern Time.

Leave Boston (via New York, New Haven and Hartford R. R.) . . . . 7.00 P. M.

JANUARY 25 and FEBRUARY 22, 1898.

Leave New York (via Pennsylvania R. R.)

	West Twenty-third Street	9.20	A. M.
	Cortlandt and Desbrosses Streets . .	9.30	"
"	Brooklyn (via Annex Boat)	9.10	"
"	Jersey City (via Pennsylvania R. R.) . .	9.44	"
"	Newark " " . .	9.58	"
"	Elizabeth " " . .	10.08	"
"	Trenton " " . .	11.09	"
"	Philadelphia " " . .	12.09	P. M.
"	Wilmington, Del. " " . .	12.49	"
"	Baltimore " " . .	2.25	"
"	Washington (via Pennsylvania and Richmond, Fredericksburg and Potomac Railroads)	3.46	P. M.

Leave Richmond (via Atlantic Coast Line) . . 7.45 "
" Petersburg, Va. " " . . 8.34 "
" So. Rocky Mount, N. C. " . . 11.37 "

JANUARY 26 and FEBRUARY 23, 1898.

Eastern Time.

Leave Florence (via Atlantic Coast Line) . . 4.51 A. M.
Arrive Ashley Junction " " . . 7.38 "

Central Time.

Arrive Ashley Junction " " . . 6.38 A. M.
Leave Ashley Junction (via Plant System) . . . 6.45 "
" Savannah " " . . . . 10.15 "
Arrive Jacksonville " " . . . 3.15 P. M.

All meals on special train will be served in the dining car.

◄●►

NORTH-BOUND SCHEDULE.

FEBRUARY 10 and MARCH 10, 1898.

Central Time.

Leave Jacksonville (via Plant System) . . . . . 9.00 A. M.
" Ashley Junction (via Atlantic Coast Line) 6.12 P. M.

FEBRUARY 11 and MARCH 11, 1898.

Eastern Time.

Arrive Richmond (via Atlantic Coast Line) . . 5.00 A. M.
Leave Richmond (via Rich., Fred. & Pot. R. R.) 5.10 "
Arrive Washington (via Pennsylvania R. R.) . . 8.45 "
    "   Baltimore   "   "   . . 10.03   "
    "   Wilmington, Del.   "   "   . . 11.45   "
    "   Philadelphia   "   "   . . 12.27 P. M.
    "   Trenton   "   "   . . 1.24   "
    "   Elizabeth   "   "   . . 2.25   "
    "   Newark   "   "   . . 2.35   "
    "   Jersey City   "   "   . . 2.49   "
    "   New York   "   "   . . 3.03   "
    "   Brooklyn (via Annex Boat) . . . . . . 3.14   "

All meals on special train will be served in the dining car.

FEBRUARY 12 and MARCH 12, 1898.

Arrive Boston (via New York, New Haven and
    Hartford R. R.) . . . . 7.00 A. M.

Via Southern Railway and Florida Central and Peninsular Railroad.

◄●►

SOUTH-BOUND SCHEDULE.

FEBRUARY 7 and MARCH 7, 1898.

Eastern Time.

Leave Boston (via New York, New Haven and
Hartford R. R.) . . . . 7.00 P. M.

FEBRUARY 8 and MARCH 8, 1898.

Leave New York (via Pennsylvania R. R.)

	West Twenty-third Street	. . . . .	9.20	A. M.
	Cortlandt and Desbrosses Streets .	.	9.30	"
"	Brooklyn (via Annex Boat)	. . . . . .	9.08	'
"	Jersey City (via Pennsylvania R. R.)	. .	9.44	'
"	Newark	"	"	. . 9.58	"
"	Elizabeth	"	"	. . 10.08	"
"	Trenton	"	"	. . 11.09	"
"	Philadelphia	"	"	. . 12.09	P. M.
"	Wilmington, Del.	"	"	. . 12.49	"
"	Baltimore	"	"	2.25	"
"	Washington (via Southern Ry.)	.	. 3.55	"
Arrive Charlottesville, Va.	"		. . . 7.02	"
Leave Charlottesville, Va.	"		. . . . 7.07	"

FEBRUARY 9 and MARCH 9, 1898.

Eastern Time.

Arrive Columbia, S. C. (via Southern Ry.) . . 6.10 A. M.

Central Time.

Arrive Columbia, S. C. (via Southern Ry.) . . 5.10 A. M.
Leave " " (via Florida Central and
Peninsular Railroad) . . . . 5.20 "
Leave Savannah " . . . . 10.05 "
Arrive Jacksonville " . . . . 3.15 P. M.

All meals on special train will be served in the dining car.

Via Southern Railway and Florida Central and Peninsular Railroad.

◄●►

NORTH-BOUND SCHEDULE.

FEBRUARY 24, 1898, tickets on the last tour being valid for return until May 31, 1898.

Central Time.

Leave Jacksonville (via Florida Central and
    Peninsular R. R.) . . . . 9.00 A. M.

Eastern Time.

Leave Columbia (via Southern Ry.) . . . . . . 7.10 P. M.

FEBRUARY 25, 1898.

Eastern Time.

Arrive Washington (via Southern Ry.)	. . . .	8.45 A. M.	
"	Baltimore (via Pennsylvania R. R.)	. . 10.03	"
"	Wilmington, Del.	"	"	. . 11.45	"
"	Philadelphia	"	"	. . 12.27 P. M.	
"	Trenton	"	"	. . 1.24	"
"	Elizabeth	"	"	. . 2.25	"
"	Newark	"	"	. . 2.35	"
"	Jersey City	"	"	. . 2.49	"
"	New York	"	"	. . 3.03	"
"	Brooklyn (via Annex Boat)	. . . . . . 3.14	"

All meals on special train will be served in the dining car.

FEBRUARY 26, 1898.

Arrive Boston (via New York, New Haven and
    Hartford R. R.) . . . . 7.00 A. M.

RESORTS.

OURISTS will be left at Jacksonville to follow their own inclinations. A few brief sketches, therefore, of the principal resorts easily accessible from Jacksonville will be found on the following pages.

JACKSONVILLE.
1002 miles from New York.

This city is the great distributing centre from which hosts of travelers pouring into the land branch out to the numberless places of interest in every direction. It is situated on the St. John's River, twenty-five miles west of the ocean, and is the largest city on the seaboard south of Savannah, and the place of first importance in business, commerce, and social life. The wide avenues of the city are shaded with grand live oaks ; rare flowers and shrubbery of the tropics adorn the grounds around the villas and hotels, and the sweet perfume of buds and blossoms permeates the air. The city is rich in suburban attractions. The drive along the St. John's River and to Riverside are especially beautiful.

The hotels of Jacksonville are numerous. Some are very handsome structures, and all offer good entertainment.

PRINCIPAL HOTELS.

The Carleton.	Hotel Oxford.	The Everett.
The Duval.	St. James Hotel.	Placide House.
The Glenada.	The Travelers.	Grand View Hotel.
	Windsor Hotel.	

BELLEAIR, FLA.

260 miles from Jacksonville, via the Plant System.

Belleair is situated on a lofty elevation, browing the waters of Clearwater Harbor, just twenty-five miles from Port Tampa, on the Mexican Gulf. Here beautiful shells, tinted and shapely, are cast upon the hard white sand. Curious fish and coral sprays sometimes find their way to

A QUIET STREAM.

these shores, and a Mediterranean shark twenty feet long, not at all a native of these waters, also drifted in with the tide. The fishing is nowhere finer, and any variety that could be obtained at famous Tarpon Springs can be caught at Belleair or Clearwater. The grouper fish, considered very fine eating, salt-water trout and Spanish mackerel, the delicious pompano and sea bass, and the mammoth tarpon are all found in season. The outdoor sports are numerous, embracing hunting, golfing, and cycling. Belleair boasts of the finest cycle track in the Southern States.

PRINCIPAL HOTEL.

The Belleview.

CEDAR KEY.

127 miles from Jacksonville, via Florida Central and Peninsular Railroad.

Cedar Key is a very popular resort for tourists and sportsmen. Many and interesting are the side trips by steamer from here. Diving for sponge is a sight well worth seeing.

PRINCIPAL HOTELS.

Bettelini House.   Schlemmer House.

CLEARWATER, FLA.

259 miles from Jacksonville, via the Plant System.

This quaint little town is situated on the west coast of Florida on one of the prettiest bays to be found on the Gulf of Mexico. About a mile and a half out across the waters lies the long, slender strip of land known as Sand Key, a natural garden of rare beauty, verdant with the dense foliage of undergrowth and crowned with the bristling, picturesque, and tousled heads of large palm trees. On the western edge of this Key extends a long beach of pure white sand, where dash the breakers of the restless, turbulent gulf.

To the east of the city lies a lake of the purest fresh water, supplied by springs. From here the town receives its water supply.

On the northern border of the town a splendid bicycle race track, paved with cement, has just been established.

Clearwater is located in one of the most attractive corners of "the land of flowers," having the advantages of level, well-paved streets and a most charming gulf drive.

PRINCIPAL HOTELS.
Verona Inn. Sea View Hotel.

DAYTONA.

51 miles from Palatka, via Florida East Coast Railway.

This town is built for about two miles along the west bank of the Halifax River. Its streets are shaded with live oaks and stately palmettos. Steamboats connect at this point for the Hillsborough and Indian Rivers.

PRINCIPAL HOTELS.
Fountain City Hotel. Palmetto Hotel. Holly Inn.
Colonnades.

DAYTONA DRIVE.

DE LAND.

110 miles from Jacksonville, via Tropical Trunk Line.

De Land is a delightfully picturesque town, situated in Volusia County, on a pine elevation. It is completely belted with extensive orange groves, and here the rich tropical productions thrive in abundance. All through this

ALONG THE ST. JOHN'S RIVER.

locality are found most picturesque lakes, on the shores of which stand beautiful residences and commodious hotels. It is a favorite spot for the sportsman—deer, turkey, and wildcat being found in abundance.

PRINCIPAL HOTELS.

The Carrolton.   College Arms.   Floral Grove Hotel.   Putnam House.

ENTERPRISE.

122 miles from Jacksonville, via Tropical Trunk Line; also reached via boat.

The advantageous situation of this town has given it a pre-eminence over many others, as it is, like its neighbor Sanford, directly on Lake Monroe—one of the headwater bodies of the St. John's.

PRINCIPAL HOTELS.
Brock House.   Live Oak House.

FERNANDINA.

36 miles from Jacksonville, via Jacksonville Branch of the Florida Central and Peninsular Railroad.

This old Spanish town was founded in 1632 by the Countess of Egmont, who essayed the culture of indigo. It has the largest and deepest harbor on the eastern coast of Florida, and during the Civil War witnessed some of the most thrilling scenes of blockade running.

Amelia Beach, over twenty miles long and two hundred feet wide, hard and firm, is one of the finest beaches in the world. The air is perfect, and the avenues broad, bowered by oak and orange.

PRINCIPAL HOTELS.
Egmont Hotel.   Florida House.

GREEN COVE SPRINGS.

30 miles from Jacksonville, via Tropical Trunk Line; also reached via boat.

The wonderful Sulphur Spring, discharging three thousand gallons of water a minute, from which the place takes its name, is located in a handsome grove of live oaks draped with Spanish moss, in the midst of wide magnolia forests. The grounds are attractively laid out in romantic walks and parks. The bathing pools are extensive, and the baths are commended not only to invalids but to all who enjoy a good plunge. Open-air bathing in December is a common everyday enjoyment.

The romantic St. David's walk extends northward along the shore two miles through the forest to Magnolia and its fine hotel. Excursions may be made by boat from here to Palatka.

PRINCIPAL HOTELS.

| Clarendon Hotel. | Oakland Hotel. | St. Clair Hotel. |
| Morganza Hotel. | Riverside House. | Hotel St. Elmo. |

THE INDIAN RIVER.

The Florida East Coast Railway extends from Jacksonville, via St. Augustine, to Miami.

The Tropical Trunk Line runs to Titusville, the head of the river, a distance of 158 miles from Jacksonville. A line of steamers runs between Titusville and Jupiter.

This river, so well known to people of the North from the fame of its oranges, is one hundred and forty-two miles

ON THE BANKS OF THE INDIAN RIVER.

in length, and in many respects one of the most remarkable and picturesque water courses in Florida. From its head, a few miles above Titusville, to the southern extremity at Jupiter Inlet, it winds through the wildest and most beautiful scenery in the State. Its width varies from one hundred feet to three miles.

LAKE WORTH.

Reached by Florida East Coast Railway, or via Tropical Trunk Line to
Titusville, where steamer is taken down the Indian River
to Jupiter, and thence via Jupiter and Lake
Worth Railway to Juno.

This beautiful lake, twenty-five miles long, with an average width of one mile, and separated by a thin strip of land from the ocean, is situated one hundred miles east and about three hundred miles south of Jacksonville.

On its shores may be seen cocoanut groves in full bearing, and some of the most palatial dwellings, in the midst of tropical gardens of wondrous beauty, reveal themselves as the steamer glides by on its transparent waters. The cocoanut industry here has become an important one, and the region has therefore become very popular with those sojourning South during the winter months, for where the cocoanut grows no stronger assurance is needed of the desirability of soil and climate. Fruits and flowers of every description bloom and ripen on its banks.

Bordering the beach of Lake Worth are the towns of Juno, Oaklawn, Lake Worth, Palm Beach, Figulus, and Hypoluxo.

In reaching Lake Worth from the Indian River the traveler passes over the "celestial railway," starting at Jupiter and terminating at Juno, with Venus and Mars sandwiched between. The road is only eight miles long, but it reaches the stars.

PRINCIPAL HOTELS (Lake Worth).

The Earman.	Hotel Royal Poinciana.	The Palms.
Delmore Cottage.	Lake Worth Hotel.	Palm Beach Inn.
	Seminole.	

BRELSFORD POINT, LAKE WORTH.

MIAMI, FLA.

366 miles from Jacksonville, via Florida East Coast Railway.

This resort is situated on Biscayne Bay, at the mouth of the Miami River. Its location, climate, and other natural advantages are all that can be desired, and it is destined to become the metropolis of South Florida. On the north bank of the Miami River stands Old Fort Dallas, which has been converted by the present owner into a luxurious home, surrounded by extensive tropical gardens in the highest state of cultivation. The town of Miami is planned to include two hundred acres on the north side and two hundred acres on the south side of the river, connected by a bridge.

PRINCIPAL HOTELS.

Connally.   Royal Palm.   Biscayne.
                     Miami.

NASSAU, N. P.

Nassau is the capital of New Providence, the chief of the Bahama Islands. It is directly east of Southern Florida, and about one hundred and fifty miles from Miami, being reached by steamer in a short sail of a few hours, through a sea landlocked most of the way. Protected by the Gulf Stream, it is absolutely free from frost and sudden changes in temperature, with a winter climate varying from sixty-eight to seventy-eight, where the variations rarely show five in twenty-four hours. The sailing is perfect, both in a landlocked harbor or on the broad Atlantic. The drives are magnificent, the roads being made out of the native stone, and for this reason it is rightly called the paradise of the cyclists. The Royal Victoria Hotel, a large four-story building, is well kept by an American. The Curry House is less pretentious, but very comfortable, and there are smaller hotels and boarding houses within the reach of every visitor. The society is excellent, and for many years Nassau has been noted for its hospitality and courtesies to Americans.

OCALA.

126 miles from Jacksonville, via Palatka and Plant System. 100 miles from Jacksonville, via Florida Central and Peninsular Railway.

Ocala is a thriving and prosperous city, the county seat of Marion, and the centre of one of the richest agricultural sections of the State, and is manifestly destined to become one of the distributing centres of the great orange belt. Near it are located extensive deposits of natural phosphates.

PRINCIPAL HOTELS.

Central Hotel.   Magnolia House.   Montezuma Hotel.
                   Ocala House.

THE OCKLAWAHA.

Starting point, Palatka, 55 miles by rail from Jacksonville, via Tropical Trunk Line.

No trip to Florida is thoroughly complete without a steamer ride up or down the Ocklawaha, for it reveals a

A ROMANTIC PATH.

29

phase of tropical scenery peculiar alone to Florida. The river is formed by a succession of swamps, springs, lakes, and lagoons.

A night journey on this river is one that cannot be rivaled for weird and beautiful effects. The pine torch headlight on the little steamer reveals masses of tangled jungle, networks of winding vines, moss, and fungi, awakens storks, cranes, herons, curlews, alligators, snakes, turtles, and a thousand other wild inmates of nature's household.

ORLANDO.

147 miles by rail or boat, via Tropical Trunk Line to Sanford, thence via Plant System. 4 miles south of Winter Park.

180 miles from Jacksonville, via Florida Central and Peninsular Railway.

Orlando is located in the midst of a region charmingly diversified by beautiful lakes, whose borders are lined with groves surrounding elegant villas and cosy winter cottage homes of Northern residents.

PRINCIPAL HOTELS.

Arcade Hotel.	Magnolia House.	Summerlin House.
Charleston House.	San Juan Hotel.	Tremont Hotel.

ORMOND, FLA.

104 miles from Jacksonville on the Florida East Coast Railway.

This beautiful little town is known as Ormond-by-the-Sea, or Ormond-on-the-Halifax—either or both—and is one of the most charming spots in Florida. The town is situated on both the east and west banks of the Halifax River, and no other locality in Florida presents such varied scenery. Halifax River is really an arm of the sea—a broad tropical lagoon, whose banks are fringed with groves of palms, orange, oak, and pine. Into it flows the Tomoka River. This picturesque stream is one of the great attractions of Florida, and an excursion from Ormond to the head of the navigable waters and return may be made in about six hours by steam or naphtha launch ; many people prefer to make the trip in sail or row boats, with which Ormond is well supplied. From the pier in front of the Hotel Ormond these craft ply their way up the Halifax, a distance of five miles, to the mouth of the Tomoka, passing beautiful rolling lands, both on the mainland and on the

WINTER BATHING IN FLORIDA.

peninsula, all under a high state of cultivation, producing oranges, vegetables of all kinds, persimmons, guavas, and other semi-tropical fruits. Three miles beyond is Thompson's Creek, "The Fisherman's Paradise." Bass, trout, mullet, carvalho, and sheepshead may here be caught in large numbers.

From the village on the west bank across the Halifax runs a long bridge, which is a favorite resort for the "fishing folk " from the hotels ; from its east end to the ocean— about a third of a mile—the road is through fragrant pines and an undulating sea of oak and palmetto, whose tops appear to form a waving carpet of green where the land rises and falls in long sea-like swells. Between the sand dunes and the sea stretches Ormond Beach—four hundred feet of yellow sand, hard and level as an asphalt pavement, and extending thirty miles without a break. It is a perfect drive, and a paradise for bicycle riders. The surf bathing of Ormond is superb, and it can be indulged in at least five days out of every seven during the winter season.

PRINCIPAL HOTELS.

| The Ormond. | Hotel Coquina. |

LAKE WORTH, AND GARDENS OF THE ROYAL POINCIANA.

PABLO BEACH.

17 miles from Jacksonville, reached by the Jacksonville and Atlantic R. R.

Directly on the Atlantic Coast, commanding a magnificent view and offering a delightfully tempered climate, is this seaboard resort of Jacksonville. It possesses one of the finest beaches in the world.

PRINCIPAL HOTELS.
Ocean House.

PALATKA.

75 miles by boat, 55 miles by rail from Jacksonville, via Tropical Trunk Line. 28 miles from St. Augustine, via Florida East Coast Railway.

This thriving and picturesque town is the centre of a large orange-growing district, and many of the most famous groves in the State are located in the vicinity. Palatka is the county seat of Putnam, and the starting point for boat excursions on the Ocklawaha and Upper St. John's Rivers. Good shooting and fishing and bathing may be enjoyed.

PRINCIPAL HOTELS.

Florida Hotel.	Hotel Graham.	Hotel Osceola.
	Putnam House.	

PUNTA GORDA.

268 miles from Jacksonville, via Plant System.

Within easy reach of the most famous tarpon fishing grounds on the coast is Punta Gorda. No more exciting sport exists than hooking one of these "game fish." Up to a few years ago it was never taken except by harpoon or seine, and to come down now and land it with a thin, silken thread line is certainly a deviation from the old school, and sport of no small account.

PRINCIPAL HOTELS.

De Soto House.	Hotel Georgia.	Hotel Southland.
	Punta Gorda Hotel.	

ROCKLEDGE.

175 miles from Jacksonville, all rail via Florida East Coast Railway,
or via Tropical Trunk Line to Titusville, thence by
boats of Indian River Steamer Line.

False Cape and Cape Canaveral throw their protecting arms far out into the sea, and shield the productive territory to the south from every chilly wind. It is in this sheltered nook that Rockledge has sprung into the prominent health and agricultural mart of to-day. It is the capital of the famous Indian River country, world-renowned for its oranges, and little less celebrated for the quantity and variety of its game. It is undoubtedly one of the most beautiful and

COCOA PALM AND ORANGE GROVE.

delightful places in Florida, and its attractions are yearly becoming better appreciated. The palmetto palm grows here in wild abundance, and the effect of avenues of these graceful trees is decidedly odd and picturesque.

PRINCIPAL HOTELS.

Hotel Indian River.   Plaza Hotel.   Rockledge House.

ST. AUGUSTINE.

First in point of historical interest of all the cities of Florida is St. Augustine, the oldest town in America. The city was founded by the Spaniards centuries ago, and many of the present inhabitants are descendants of the original grandees. It savors yet decidedly of the Spanish, and the quaint, old, balconied houses, narrow, winding streets, the ruins of the old walls, and the city gates, combine to form an old-world picture strangely in contrast with the newness of to-day. The natural advantages of St. Augustine are many. It enjoys a well-founded reputation for healthfulness, and possesses a magnificent beach, on which sea-bathing may be indulged in from the year's beginning to its end. Its grand possibilities have attracted the attention of capitalists, who have erected three of the most superb hotels in the world. These palaces, the Ponce de Leon, Cordova, and Alcazar, are built of coquina, a curious shell formation. The architecture is Spanish Renaissance and

PONCE DE LEON GATEWAY, ST. AUGUSTINE.

Mooresque ; the decorations and ornamentations are wrought
in the same spirit, and the furnishing is in keeping with the
skill which designed and the taste that executed the grand
piles. They have no equals in the world, and yet they
harmonize most happily with their antique surroundings.
Other attractive features of the old town are the sea wall,
the old slave market, the Huguenot Cemetery, the Plaza
de la Constitution, and the Castle of San Marco, now become Fort Marion.

PRINCIPAL HOTELS.

Ponce de Leon Hotel.	Florida House.	Pasade la Plaza Hotel.
The Alcazar.	Hernandez Hotel.	The St. George.
American House.	Hotel Cordova.	Lynn's Hotel.
The Barcelona.	Magnolia Hotel.	The Buckingham.
Carleton Hotel.	Ocean View Hotel.	Lorillard Villa.
Cleveland House.	The Abbey.	The Valencia.
	The Algonquin.	

SANFORD.

125 miles from Jacksonville, via Tropical Trunk Line ; also reached
by boat on St. John's River.

Sanford was originally a Spanish grant, and passed from
hand to hand until 1870, when it was purchased by Gen.
H. S. Sanford, through whose instrumentality a number
of Swedish families were imported, and to their toil and
industry the prosperity of the present community is largely
due.

The picturesque body of Lake Monroe, on whose shore
it is partly built, adds no small share to the attractive
features of the place. It has long been held in the high
estimation of Florida tourists and well warrants a visit.

PRINCIPAL HOTELS.

Sanford House.	Sirrine Hotel.	San Leon Hotel.

SILVER SPRINGS.

100 miles from Jacksonville, on the Florida Central and Peninsular
Railroad ; also reached via Palatka and the Plant System.

Silver Springs is well known to all who have heard of
Florida. This vast circular basin, six hundred feet in diam-
eter and nearly fifty feet in depth, is the source of a
river known as Silver Spring Run, navigable for small

PALMETTO GROVE.

steamboats, and which empties into the Ocklawaha River,
about nine miles distant, and is really one of the greatest
of natural wonders. So transparent is the water that peb-
bles and sand can be seen distinctly at the bottom.

This place is owned and cultivated by the Florida Central and Peninsular Railroad, and is one of the prettiest
places in Florida.

This crystal pool, supposed to have been Ponce de Leon's fountain of perpetual youth, is reached via rail or by boat up the Ocklawaha River from Palatka to Silver Spring Run, a swift and pellucid stream. From the springs Ocala, six miles distant, can be reached by railway or via a magnificent bicycle path.

TALLAHASSEE.

165 miles from Jacksonville, via Florida Central and Peninsular Railroad.

It is the capital of the State and a source of pride to all Floridians. It is beautifully built on a high elevation, and the design of the broad streets and avenues, shaded with evergreens and live oaks, and the bountiful and luxurious growth of flowers and shrubs, make it a veritable garden spot.

Here is the Lafayette Land Grant, and the noted lakes swarming with ducks and brant. The Murat residence, and the grave of Prince Achille Murat, son of the King of Naples, and a hundred and one places, may be visited and enjoyed to the profit of the tourist. Among these is the celebrated Wauklilla Spring, fourteen miles south of the city, reached by carriage or saddle, and which is the rival in area and depth to the great Silver Spring near Ocala.

PRINCIPAL HOTELS.

Baldwin House.   New Leon Hotel.   St. James Hotel.

TAMPA.

212 miles from Jacksonville, via Florida Central and Peninsular Railroad.
240 miles from Jacksonville, via Tropical Trunk Line to
Sanford and Plant System.

The run from Jacksonville to Tampa via Sanford is not without interest, as the passenger traverses Winter Park, Orlando, and the high pine lands to the Kissimmee Lake district, and thence on to that fertile and productive country where the town stakes of Tampa were first driven.

Here cotton, corn, rice, sugar cane, orange, lime, lemon, banana, and all the fruits of the tropical zone grow in profusion. Its seaport and mercantile value give it a prominent place among the cities of the State, and as a winter refuge it is not surpassed by any point on the Gulf Coast. The great Tampa Bay Hotel is the largest in the South, and is a marvel of luxurious appointments and lavish outlay. Port Tampa, nine miles south of Tampa, is the terminus of the Plant System of Railroads. It is situated on the shores of Tampa Bay, and from its wharves the steamers sail for Havana and Jamaica. The "Inn" at Port Tampa is located immediately upon the long pier, and is a very agreeable stopping place *en route* to or from Key West and Cuba.

PRINCIPAL HOTELS.

The Almeria.	The De Soto.	Tampa House.
City Hotel.	Tampa Bay Hotel.	The Inn (Port Tampa).

ON TAMPA BAY.

PATH BY LAKE WORTH.

TARPON SPRINGS.

121 miles from Sanford, via Plant System.

202 miles from Jacksonville, via Florida Central and Peninsular Railroad, via Lacoochee and the Plant System.

Foremost among the many attractive winter towns which have come into influential life along the Gulf coast is Tarpon Springs. The rapid clearing and building of this South Florida town would surprise some of the Western land boomers. It has the advantage of situation, the warm winds from the Gulf waters, whose power works wonders, and orange groves of number and great yield.

PRINCIPAL HOTEL.

Tarpon Springs Hotel.

WINTER PARK.

143 miles from Jacksonville, via Tropical Trunk Line to Sanford, and thence via Plant System; also via Florida Central and Peninsular Railroad.

When one considers that this resort, known to-day all over the States and abroad, was in 1881 a complete wilderness, it shows with what rapidity towns and cities are born in this wonderful country of ours. It is a picturesque town, laid out in the shape of a Greek cross, bordering on the shores of a chain of pretty lakes. The region immediately surrounding is highly productive of oranges. It is undoubtedly one of the best known and most highly esteemed winter homes in the far South, being extremely healthful. The noted Seminole Hotel, built in the most artistic and modern style, is alive with the gayety and life of a migratory people under its rich and hospitable roof.

PRINCIPAL HOTELS.

Seminole Hotel.   Rogers House.

This list could be extended to great length, and then perhaps all the attractive places would not secure mention. The sketches are intended as brief introductions to the most prominent places that typify the distinctive life and characteristics of this wonderful land, with its earth, air, and water forming nature's most perfect sanitarium, where thousands are restored to health and strength. The romantic Spaniard who sought the fount of perpetual youth here exercised excellent judgment.

If the hand-book serves to direct the steps of the tourist into pleasant paths, its purpose will have been achieved.

INDEX.

CALIFORNIA.

•

FOUR PERSONALLY-CONDUCTED TOURS

TO THE

GOLDEN GATE

Will be run during the winter and spring of 1898.

The first will leave Boston January 7, New York and Philadelphia January 8. $340.00 from Boston ; $335.00 from New York and Philadelphia, and other points on Pennsylvania Railroad System ; $330.00 from Pittsburg.

The second will leave Boston January 26, and New York and Philadelphia January 27. $315.00 from Boston ; $310.00 from New York, Philadelphia, and all other points on the Pennsylvania Railroad System ; $305.00 from Pittsburg.

The third will leave Boston February 15, and New York and Philadelphia February 16. $340.00 from Boston ; $335.00 from New York, Philadelphia, and all other points on the Pennsylvania Railroad System ; $330.00 from Pittsburg.

The fourth tour will leave Boston March 18, and New York and Philadelphia March 19. For this tour tickets will be sold covering all features on going trip, and transportation returning by regular trains, at rate of $220.20 from Boston, $208.20 from New York, and $205.20 from Philadelphia. Tickets will also be sold to include transportation on going trip only at rate of $148.75 from Boston, $141.75 from New York, and $140.25 from Philadelphia.

The rates for these tours are as low as is consistent with the best service.

PENNSYLVANIA RAILROAD TOURS.

— •

WASHINGTON.

A series of short personally-conducted tours from NEW YORK, PHILADELPHIA, and adjacent points will be run

DECEMBER 28, 1897;

JANUARY 13, 1898;

FEBRUARY 3, 1898;

MARCH 3 and 31, 1898;

APRIL 21, 1898;

MAY 12, 1898.

Rates, including transportation and two days' accommodation at the best Washington hotels:—

$14.50 from New York, Brooklyn, and Newark;

$13.50 from Trenton, and

$11.50 from Philadelphia.

Proportionate rates from other points.

TOURS TO
OLD POINT COMFORT, VA.,
RICHMOND, VA., AND
WASHINGTON, D. C.

FEBRUARY 19, MARCH 16, and APRIL 7, 1898.

RATES:

From New York, Brooklyn, and Newark $35 00
From Trenton, N. J. 34 00
From Philadelphia 32 50
    Covering all expenses for a period of six days.
    Proportionate rates from other stations.

•

TOURS TO
OLD POINT COMFORT AND WASHINGTON.

DECEMBER 28, 1897;
JANUARY 29, 1898;
APRIL 23, 1898.

RATES:

From New York, Brooklyn, and Newark $22 00
From Trenton 21 00
From Philadelphia 19 50
    Covering all expenses for a period of four days.
    Proportionate rates from other stations.

TOURS TO
OLD POINT COMFORT AND VIRGINIA BEACH.

·

December 28, 1897;

January 29, 1898;

February 19, 1898;

March 19, 1898;

April 7 and 23, 1898.

RATES TO OLD POINT COMFORT:

From New York, Brooklyn, and Newark $16 00

From Trenton 15 00

From Philadelphia 14 00

Covering transportation in each direction.

Proportionate rates from other stations.

Tickets good to return within six days.

Luncheon going and one and three-fourths days' board at Old Point Comfort.

$4.00 additional to Virginia Beach, including one day's board at the Princess Anne Hotel.

BOSTON TO WASHINGTON TOURS.

·

For the winter and spring of 1897-8 the Pennsylvania Railroad Company will run seven personally-conducted trips to Washington. These are unquestionably the most popular short tours that are given under the auspices of this Company, and especially appeal to the residents of Boston and New England in general.

The dates selected are:—

THURSDAY, DECEMBER 2, 1897;

THURSDAY, JANUARY 13, 1898;

THURSDAY, FEBRUARY 10, 1898;

THURSDAY, MARCH 10, 1898;

FRIDAY, APRIL 1, 1898;

(Seven days, all rail.)

THURSDAY, APRIL 28, 1898;

THURSDAY, MAY 19, 1898.

The low rate of $25.00 will apply to all these tours.

This includes accommodations at the best hotels in Washington, and all necessary expenses.

www.ingramcontent.com/pod-product-compliance
Lightning Source LLC
Chambersburg PA
CBHW021439090426
42739CB00009B/1554